Low Fat Breakfast

----- ✌🙰🙰✌ -----

Discover The Most Delicious Low Fat Breakfast Recipes And Healthy Smoothie Recipes To Kick-Start Your Day

Table of Contents

Introduction iii

Chapter 1: Low Fat Smoothie.................................... 1

    Banana Ginger Smoothie.................................... 1

    Orange Cream Delight 1

    Green Tea With Blueberry And Banana Smoothie 2

    Very Berry Smoothie.......................................3

    Mama's Delight 3

    Passionate Pineapple 4

    Kiwi and Strawberry Drink.................................4

    BBS Smoothie 4

    Papaya Passion 5

    Peach Passion 5

    Apricot and Mango Mania.................................. 6

    Watermelon Woozy 7

    Berry Smoothie Delight 7

    Early Morning Sunrise....................................8

    Vanilla and Berry Smoothie...............................8

    Delicious Dilemma 9

    Luscious Smoothie..9

    Ice Cream Smoothie 10

    Peachy Smoothie.. 10

    Orangey Delight Smoothie 11

    Banana Peanut Butter Smoothie 11

    Blueberry Blast Smoothie...............................11

    Coconut Smoothie with added Fruits..................... 12

Tropical Smoothie 12

Ginger Green Tea Smoothie... 13

Honeydew Smoothie 14

Kefir Smoothie 14

Buttermilk and Mango Strawberry Smoothie 14

Soy Milk Smoothie 15

Mango Obsession 15

Smooth Nutty Smoothie.. 16

Healthy Herby Smoothie 16

Apple Smoothie 17

Chapter 2:Other Low Fat Breakfast Recipes............. 19

South Western Omelette... 19

French toast... 20

Breakfast muffins 21

Three Grain Cereal 22

Tostada 23

Mashed Potato Omelette.. 24

Breakfast Casseroles..25

Low fat Delight 26

Healthy Crepes 26

Leek Bacon Tart 27

Spanish Omelette 29

Spinach Omelette 30

Frittatas with Smoked Gouda 31

Breakfast braid 32

Whole Wheat Pancakes.. 33

Sunny Frittatas 34

Conclusion 35

iii

Introduction

We all know that breakfast is the most important meal of the day, yet more often than not most of us end up skipping breakfast. The main reason for this is the fact that most of us hate to eat the boring and drab cereals that are healthy but tasteless.

What if I said that healthy and tasty can go hand in hand for your breakfast? Well yes, absolutely. Now you can have a sumptuous breakfast, which is easy to make, refreshing, low fat and also tasty.

Made from fresh ingredients, these recipes are extremely easy to make and are much better in the taste department than boring cereal.

So why wait? Let's get started.

© **Copyright 2014 by Wendy Adamson - All rights reserved.**

This document is geared towards providing exact and reliable information in regards to the topic and issue covered. The publication is sold with the idea that the publisher is not required to render accounting, officially permitted, or otherwise, qualified services. If advice is necessary, legal or professional, a practiced individual in the profession should be ordered.

- From a Declaration of Principles which was accepted and approved equally by a Committee of the American Bar Association and a Committee of Publishers and Associations.

In no way is it legal to reproduce, duplicate, or transmit any part of this document in either electronic means or in printed format. Recording of this publication is strictly prohibited and any storage of this document is not allowed unless with written permission from the publisher. All rights reserved.

The information provided herein is stated to be truthful and consistent, in that any liability, in terms of inattention or otherwise, by any usage or abuse of any policies, processes, or directions contained within is the solitary and utter responsibility of the recipient reader. Under no circumstances will any legal responsibility or blame be held against the publisher for any reparation, damages, or monetary loss due to the information herein, either directly or indirectly.

Respective authors own all copyrights not held by the publisher.

The information herein is offered for informational purposes solely, and is universal as so. The presentation of the information is without contract or any type of guarantee assurance.

The trademarks that are used are without any consent, and the publication of the trademark is without permission or backing by the trademark owner. All trademarks and brands within this book are for clarifying purposes only and are the owned by the owners themselves, not affiliated with this document.

Chapter 1:

Low Fat Smoothie

Banana Ginger Smoothie

Ingredients

- 2 bananas, sliced
- 1 cup vanilla yoghurt
- 1 tablespoon honey
- 3/4 teaspoon ginger, freshly grated

Method

1. Add all the ingredients one by one in a blender and blend till smooth for a couple of minutes
2. Serve chilled in a tall glass.

Orange Cream Delight

Ingredients

- 1 orange, peeled
- 1/4 cup fat free yoghurt

Chapter 1: Low Fat Smoothie

- 2 tablespoons orange juice concentrate, frozen
- 1/4 teaspoon vanilla extract
- Ice cubes

Method

1. Add all the ingredients one by one in a blender and blend till smooth for a couple of minutes
2. Serve chilled in a tall glass.

Green Tea With Blueberry And Banana Smoothie

Ingredients

- 3 tablespoons water
- 1 bag green tea
- 2 teaspoon honey
- 1 cup blueberries, frozen
- 1 banana, small
- 3/4 cup soy milk

Method

1. Heat water till it gets steaming hot. Dip the tea bag in the water and brew for 3 minutes. Take it out and stir in the honey
2. In a blender jar add all the ingredients (except tea mixture) one by one and blend till smooth.
3. Add the tea mixture to the blender and blend once again.
4. Serve chilled in a tall glass.

Very Berry Smoothie

Ingredients

- 1 cup raspberries, frozen
- 3/4 cup almond milk
- 1/4 cup pitted cherries
- 2 tablespoons honey
- 2 teaspoon grated ginger, fresh
- 1 teaspoon flaxseed, ground
- 2 teaspoon lemon juice, freshly squeezed

Method

1. Add all the ingredients one by one in a blender and blend till smooth for a couple of minutes
2. Serve chilled in a tall glass.

Mama's Delight

Ingredients

- 1 cup yoghurt, non-fat
- 1 banana
- 1/2 cup orange juice
- 6 small strawberries, frozen

Method

1. Add all the ingredients one by one in a blender and blend till smooth for a couple of minutes
2. Serve chilled in a tall glass.

Chapter 1: Low Fat Smoothie

Passionate Pineapple

Ingredients

- 1 cup vanilla yoghurt
- 1 cup pineapple pieces
- Ice cubes

Method

1. Add all the ingredients one by one in a blender and blend till smooth for a couple of minutes
2. Serve chilled in a tall glass.

Kiwi and Strawberry Drink

Ingredients

- 1 banana, ripe and sliced
- 1 1/4 cup apple juice, chilled
- 1 kiwifruit, sliced
- 2 teaspoons honey
- 6 strawberries, frozen

Method

1. Add all the ingredients one by one in a blender and blend till smooth for a couple of minutes
2. Serve chilled in a tall glass.

BBS Smoothie

Ingredients

- 2 cups soy milk, light

4

- 1 cup blueberries, frozen
- 1 banana, frozen and sliced
- 1 tsp honey
- 2 teaspoon vanilla extract

Method

1. Add all the ingredients one by one in a blender and blend till smooth for a couple of minutes
2. You can add more milk for a thinner consistency
3. Serve chilled in a tall glass.

Papaya Passion

Ingredients

- 1 small papaya, chopped
- 1 cup plain yoghurt
- 1/2 cup pineapple chunks
- 1 teaspoon coconut extract
- 1 teaspoon flaxseed, ground

Method

1. Add all the ingredients one by one in a blender and blend till smooth for a couple of minutes
2. Serve chilled in a tall glass.

Peach Passion

Ingredients

- 1 cup milk

Chapter 1: Low Fat Smoothie

- 2 tablespoons vanilla yoghurt
- 1 cup strawberries
- 1 cup peaches, frozen
- 2 teaspoons protein powder
- 1 pinch powdered ginger
- 3 ice cubes

Method

1. Add all the ingredients one by one in a blender and blend till smooth for a couple of minutes
2. Serve chilled in a tall glass.

Apricot and Mango Mania

Ingredients

- 6 fresh apricots, chopped, peeled and stone removed
- 2 ripe mangoes, peeled and chopped
- 4 teaspoon lemon juice
- 1 cup plain fat yoghurt
- 1/8 teaspoon vanilla extract
- Lemon peels
- Ice cubes

Method

1. In a blender jar add all the ingredients (except lemon peel) one by one and blend till smooth.
2. Serve chilled in a tall glass and decorate with the lemon peel.

Watermelon Woozy

Ingredients

- 2 cups watermelon, chopped
- 1/4 cup milk, fat free
- 2 cups ice

Method

1. Add all the ingredients one by one in a blender and blend till smooth for a couple of minutes
2. Serve chilled in a tall glass.

Berry Smoothie Delight

Ingredients

- 2 cup strawberries, chopped
- 1 cup blueberries
- 1 cup raspberries
- 2 tablespoons honey
- 1 teaspoon lemon juice
- Ice cubes

Method

1. Add all the ingredients one by one in a blender and blend till smooth for a couple of minutes
2. Serve chilled in a tall glass.

Chapter 1: Low Fat Smoothie

Early Morning Sunrise

Ingredients

- 1 cup apricot nectar, chilled
- 1 banana
- 1/4 cup club soda
- 1 cup low fat peach yoghurt
- 1 tablespoon lemonade concentrate

Method

1. Add all the ingredients one by one in a blender and blend till smooth for a couple of minutes
2. When ready to serve add the club soda and serve immediately.

Vanilla and Berry Smoothie

Ingredients

- 1 cup unsweetened apricots, frozen
- 1 cup unsweetened strawberries, frozen
- 1 cup pineapple juice, unsweetened
- 1 cup fat free yoghurt

Method

1. Add all the ingredients one by one in a blender and blend till smooth for a couple of minutes
2. Serve chilled in a tall glass.

Delicious Dilemma

Ingredients

- 1 cup mixed frozen berries
- 1 cup canned crushed pineapple juice
- 1 cup yoghurt
- 1 cup ripe banana
- 1 cup orange juice

Method

1. Add all the ingredients one by one in a blender and blend till smooth for a couple of minutes
2. Serve chilled in a tall glass.

Luscious Smoothie

Ingredients

- 1 cup strawberries, frozen and unsweetened
- 1 cup milk, skimmed
- 1 tablespoon flaxseed oil
- 1 tablespoon sunflower seeds

Method

1. Add all the ingredients one by one in a blender and blend till smooth for a couple of minutes
2. Serve chilled in a tall glass.

Chapter 1: Low Fat Smoothie

Ice Cream Smoothie

Ingredients

- 1 cup mixed berries, frozen
- 1/2 cup flavoured yoghurt
- 1/2 cup orange juice

Method

1. Add all the ingredients one by one in a blender and blend till smooth for a couple of minutes
2. Serve chilled in a tall glass.

Peachy Smoothie

Ingredients

- 1/2 cup low fat milk
- 1/2 cup yoghurt
- 1 cup frozen peaches
- Honey to taste
- Vanilla extract to taste
- Cinnamon to taste
- Nutmeg to taste
- Ginger to taste

Method

1. Add all the ingredients one by one in a blender and blend till smooth for a couple of minutes
2. Serve chilled in a tall glass.

Low Fat Breakfast

Orangey Delight Smoothie

Ingredients

- 1 cup orange juice
- Lime juice
- 1 cup strawberries
- 1 banana, ripe

Method

1. Add all the ingredients one by one in a blender and blend till smooth for a couple of minutes
2. Serve chilled in a tall glass.

Banana Peanut Butter Smoothie

Ingredients

- 1 banana, ripe chopped, preferably frozen
- 1/2 cup milk
- 1/4 cup yoghurt
- 1 1/2 cup peanut butter

Method

1. Add all the ingredients one by one in a blender and blend till smooth for a couple of minutes
2. Serve chilled in a tall glass.

Blueberry Blast Smoothie

Ingredients

- 1 cup low fat milk

11

Chapter 1: Low Fat Smoothie

- 1/2 cup yoghurt
- 1 cup blueberries
- Honey
- 1 teaspoon Pomegranate seeds

Method
1. Add all the ingredients one by one in a blender and blend till smooth for a couple of minutes
2. Serve chilled in a tall glass.

Coconut Smoothie with added Fruits

Ingredients
- Coconut water
- 2 bananas
- 1/2 Greek yoghurt
- 2 mangoes, small
- 1 tsp Honey

Method
1. Make ice cubes of coconut water.
2. Chop the fruits in uneven chunks.
3. Add all the ingredients one by one in a blender and blend till smooth for a couple of minutes and serve.

Tropical Smoothie

Ingredients
- 2 cups soy milk

Low Fat Breakfast

- 2 ounce tofu chunks
- 1/2 cup papaya chunks, frozen
- 1/2 cup chopped pineapple, frozen
- 1/2 cup chopped mango, frozen
- 1 tsp Honey
- Vanilla extract

Method

1. Add all the ingredients one by one in a blender and blend till smooth for a couple of minutes
2. Serve chilled in a tall glass.

Ginger Green Tea Smoothie

Ingredients

- 2 cups peaches, frozen
- 1/2 cup flavoured peach Greek yoghurt
- 1 green Tea bag
- Honey
- Grated ginger to taste
- Water

Method

1. Boil a cup of water and dip the tea bag in it and let it brew.
2. Add all the ingredients one by one in a blender and blend till smooth for a couple of minutes
3. Serve chilled in a tall glass.

Chapter 1: Low Fat Smoothie

Honeydew Smoothie

Ingredients

- 2 cups honeydew melon, chopped
- 1 cup almond milk
- 1 ice cube
- Honey to taste

Method

1. Add all the ingredients one by one in a blender and blend till smooth for a couple of minutes
2. Serve chilled in a tall glass.

Kefir Smoothie

Ingredients

- Ice
- 1/2 cup Kefir
- 3/4 cup diced pineapple
- Honey to taste

Method

1. Add all the ingredients one by one in a blender and blend till smooth for a couple of minutes
2. Serve chilled in a tall glass.

Buttermilk and Mango Strawberry Smoothie

Ingredients

- 1 pound ripe strawberries

14

- 1 large, ripe mango
- 1 small ripe banana, frozen
- 1 6-ounce pot fat-free vanilla yoghurt
- 1 cup low fat buttermilk
- 2 tablespoon honey

Method

1. Chop the fruits in small pieces and put them in a blender.
2. Add the honey, yogurt and buttermilk and blend for about 2 minutes or till the mix gets frothy.
3. Serve cold

Soy Milk Smoothie

Ingredients

- 1 cup vanilla soy milk
- 1/2 cup blueberries, frozen
- 1/2 cups cereals
- 1 banana, frozen and sliced

Method

1. Add all the ingredients one by one in a blender and blend till smooth for a couple of minutes
2. Serve chilled in a tall glass.

Mango Obsession

Ingredients

- 1 can packed pineapple chunks

Chapter 1: Low Fat Smoothie

- 1 large mango, ripe, peeled and chopped
- 1 cup vanilla yoghurt
- 1 ripe banana, chopped
- Ice cubes

Method

1. Add all the ingredients one by one in a blender and blend till smooth for a couple of minutes
2. Serve chilled in a tall glass.

Smooth Nutty Smoothie

Ingredients

- 1 tablespoon walnut,
- 1 cup milk, skimmed
- 1 tablespoon almond
- Honey according to taste
- 1 tablespoon cashew, unsalted
- 1 tablespoon sunflower seeds

Method

1. Add all the ingredients one by one in a blender and blend till smooth for a couple of minutes
2. Serve chilled in a tall glass.

Healthy Herby Smoothie

Ingredients

- 1 tablespoon holy basil leaves

16

Low Fat Breakfast

- 1 cup milk, skimmed
- 1 tablespoon rose essence
- Rose Petals

Method

1. Add all the ingredients one by one in a blender and blend till smooth for a couple of minutes
2. Serve chilled in a tall glass.

Apple Smoothie

Ingredients

- 1 cup green apple diced
- 1 cup milk, skimmed
- 1 cup red apple diced
- Vanilla extract

Method

1. Add all the ingredients one by one in a blender and blend till smooth for a couple of minutes
2. Serve chilled in a tall glass.

Chapter 2:

Other Low Fat Breakfast Recipes

South Western Omelette

Ingredients

- 2 tablespoons cilantro, chopped
- 1 large egg
- 4 egg whites
- Salt
- 1/2 cup black beans, rinsed and drained
- 1/4 cup green onions, chopped
- 1/4 cup cheddar cheese, reduced-fat
- 1/4 cup bottled salsa
- Oil

Method

1. In a large bowl add the egg, egg white, cilantro and salt and whisk well.
2. Add beans, cheese, salsa and onions in another bowl and mix them well
3. Heat non-stick skillet and grease it with some oil.

Chapter 2: Other Low Fat Breakfast Recipes

4. Slowly ladle out some of the egg mixture on the pan.

5. Let it set slightly and then lightly tilting the pan let the runaway mixture settle under the cooked portion.

6. Cook for some time and then flip.

7. Put the bean mixture on one half of the omelette. Carefully fold the other side onto this.

8. Cook till the cheese melts.

9. Serve hot.

French toast

Ingredients

- 3/4 cup non-fat milk
- 1/2 cup egg substitute
- 1/2 teaspoon cinnamon
- 2 teaspoon vanilla extract
- 8 slices whole grain bread, preferably a day old

Method

1. In a bowl mix the egg substitute, vanilla, milk and cinnamon and whisk.

2. Take the bread slices and dip it in the mixture so that both the sides get soaked properly.

3. Heat a non-stick pan and grease it with some oil.

4. Once the oil is hot enough, place the bread slices on the pan and brown them from both sides.

5. Garnish with maple syrup.

Low Fat Breakfast

Breakfast muffins

Ingredients

- 1 1/2 cups all-purpose flour
- 1/2 cup oats
- 1 teaspoon baking soda
- 1 teaspoon baking powder
- Salt
- 1/2 teaspoon ginger
- 1/2 teaspoon cinnamon
- 1/4 teaspoon nutmeg
- 1/2 cup firmly packed brown sugar
- 1/4 cup canola oil
- 1 egg, lightly beaten
- 1 teaspoon vanilla extract
- 1 8-ounce can crushed pineapple
- 1/2 cup fat-free milk
- 1/2 cup raisins
- 1 1/2 cups freshly grated carrots

Method

1. Keep the oven on preheat mode on 350 degrees. Grease a muffin tray or put paper liners in it.
2. In a bowl mix the flour, baking powder, soda, oats, salt, ginger, nutmeg and cinnamon.
3. Take another bowl and mix egg, sugar, oil, milk and vanilla extract.
4. Add carrots, pineapple and raisin to the liquid mixture.
5. In a separate bowl combine the wet and the dry mixture

Chapter 2: Other Low Fat Breakfast Recipes

until it combines well.

6. Pour this into muffin cups till they are 3/4 full.

7. Bake for 20 minutes.

Three Grain Cereal

Ingredients

- 1/2 cup maple syrup
- 3 tablespoons canola oil
- 1/3 cup honey
- 4 1/2 cups regular oats
- 1 1/2 tablespoons vanilla extract
- 3/4 cup chopped walnuts or pecans
- 1/2 cup wheat germ
- 1 cup uncooked quick-cooking barley
- 1/4 teaspoon ground nutmeg
- 1 teaspoon ground cinnamon
- Cooking spray
- 1 cup mixed dried fruits

Method

1. Keep the oven on preheat mode on 325 degrees Fahrenheit.

2. In a bowl mix maple syrup, honey, canola oil and vanilla extract. Whisk it.

3. In another large bowl mix oats, walnuts, barley, wheat germ, nutmeg and cinnamon. Add the syrup mix and combine both the mixes well.

4. Spread this mixture on a greased jelly-roll pan.

Low Fat Breakfast

5. Bake for 30 minutes, stirring every 10 minutes and then garnish with the dried fruits.

6. Cool and serve.

Tostada

Ingredients

- 1/4 cup low-fat milk
- 2 large eggs
- 1/8 teaspoon ground black pepper
- Salt
- 4 large egg whites $
- 4 corn tortillas
- 1/4 cup chopped green onions
- 1/2 cup cheddar cheese
- 1 cup canned black beans, rinsed and drained
- 1/4 cup sour cream
- 1/2 cup bottled salsa

Method

1. In a large glass bowl mix the milk, eggs, egg whites and salt and pepper. Whisk it all well till it gets frothy.

2. On a hot girdle, fry the mixture till it gets done (scramble)

3. On a microwave safe plate place the tortillas and put the above mixture on them.

4. Add cheese, beans and onions.

5. Microwave on high mode for half a minute.

6. Garnish with sour cream and salsa.

Chapter 2: Other Low Fat Breakfast Recipes

Mashed Potato Omelette

Ingredients

- 1 medium potato
- 1 tablespoon minced chives
- Salt
- Freshly ground black pepper
- 4 large eggs
- 1 large egg white
- 1 garlic clove, minced
- 1 tablespoon olive oil
- 1 teaspoon extra-virgin olive oil
- 3 tablespoons Manchego cheese
- 1/2 cup halved cherry tomatoes

Method

1. Keep the oven on preheating mode at 350 degree Fahrenheit.

2. Heat some water in a saucepan and let the potatoes boil. Simmer for 20 minutes. Cool and peel them and slice it.

3. In a bowl mix chives, salt, pepper, eggs and egg whites and whisk.

4. In a non-stick pan heat a teaspoon of oil and then add garlic and the boiled and sliced potatoes. Sprinkle some salt.

5. Slowly mash the potatoes so as to form a layer at the bottom of the pan. Pour the egg mixture over this layer. Cook for a minute.

6. Stir the mixture gently and press the potato to the bottom once again. Cook for a couple of minutes. Remove from heat.

Low Fat Breakfast

7. Sprinkle cheese over this.

8. Bake this in the oven for 7 minutes.

9. Drizzle olive oil over this and then gently take this off from the pan and serve.

10. Garnish with tomatoes and chives.

Breakfast Casseroles

Ingredients

- 12 ounces turkey breakfast sausage
- 2 cups low-fat milk
- 2 cups egg substitute
- Ground black pepper
- 1 teaspoon dry mustard
- Salt
- 1/4 teaspoon ground red pepper
- 3 large eggs
- 16 slices bread
- 1 cup cheddar cheese, shredded
- Oil

Method

1. Grease a pan with oil and heat it on medium flame. Add the sausage to IT and cook till it gets brown. Crumble the sausage while cooking. When done remove from heat and keep aside.

2. In a bowl mix milk, egg substitute, salt and pepper, red chillies and mustard and whisk it together.

3. Cut the crust of the bread and dice them in 1 inch cubes.

Chapter 2: Other Low Fat Breakfast Recipes

One by one add these cubes, sausage and cheese to the milk and egg mixture and stir it slowly.

4. Pour this mixture in a greased baking tray. Spread the mixture evenly and cover it. Put this mixture in the refrigerator overnight.

5. Keep the oven on preheat mode at 350 degrees Fahrenheit.

6. Remove the casserole and thaw it for 30 minutes.

7. Sprinkle paprika over the casserole and bake at 350 degrees for 45 minutes or till done.

8. Keep aside for 10 minutes and serve.

Low fat Delight

Ingredients

- 1 large sliced banana
- 1 cup sliced strawberries
- 2 cups low fat granola
- 2 cups strawberry yoghurt

Method

1. Take glasses or goblets and layer the four ingredients alternatively.

2. Garnish with sliced strawberries.

3. Chill before serving.

Healthy Crepes

Ingredients

- 1/2 cup all-purpose flour

Low Fat Breakfast

- Salt
- 2/3 cup milk
- 1 egg, lightly beaten

Method

1. Take a bowl and add the flour and salt to it and mix it well. Make a small depression in between and break the egg in the centre
2. Whisk the mixture and while doing so slowly add milk to it.
3. Mix properly; the batter should not have lumps. Set aside for 5 minutes.
4. Grease a pan and heat it for a bit. Pour some of the batter on the pan making it as thin as possible. Flip when done on one side.
5. Repeat to make more.
6. Serve with jam or chocolate sauce or a garnish of your choice.

Leek Bacon Tart

Ingredients

Crust:

- 1 cup all-purpose flour
- Salt
- 2 tablespoons butter
- 2 tablespoons vegetable shortening
- 4 tablespoons ice water
- 1/4 teaspoon cider vinegar

27

Chapter 2: Other Low Fat Breakfast Recipes

Filling:

- 3 bacon slices, cut into thin strips
- 7 cups chopped leek
- Salt
- Black pepper
- 1 1/4 cups egg substitute
- 2/3 cup milk

Method

Crust

1. In a bowl mix flour and salt. Whisk. Chop the butter and shortenings to make coarse mix. Add this to the flour and mix.
2. Slowly add water and vinegar and mix. Make sure that you add this slowly, 1 tablespoon at a time. Form firm dough.
3. Put this dough in a cling wrap and cover it on top with another wrap. Now with a rolling pin roll a 12 inch circle. Keep aside.
4. Keep the oven on preheat mode at 425 degrees F.
5. Remove the top wrap and let the dough stand.
6. Put the dough in a greased baking pan and remove the bottom wrap. Bake for 10 minutes at 425 degrees.
7. Keep aside to cool.

Filling

1. Heat milk in a large pan till it gets considerably hot.
2. Put bacon in this and cook for 5 minutes. Remove bacon and add leek. Cover and cook for 20 minutes.
3. Add salt and pepper. Stir occasional and remove from pan.

Low Fat Breakfast

4. Arrange the leek and bacon on the crust.

5. In a bowl mix egg substitute, salt and pepper and whisk. Pour this on the crust.

6. Bake for 25 minutes at 425 degrees.

7. Serve after 10 minutes.

Spanish Omelette

Ingredients

- 1 1/2 cups sliced potato
- 1 garlic clove, minced
- 1/2 cup chopped red bell pepper
- 1/2 cup chopped onion
- 1/4 cup sliced pitted green olives
- Oregano
- 1/2 cup mozzarella cheese, shredded
- 8 large egg whites
- 4 large eggs
- Salt
- Pepper
- 1/2 teaspoon olive oil
- Oil

Method

1. Boil a potato, once done peel it and dice. Keep aside.

2. Heat another skillet and grease it. Add onion, garlic, bell pepper and potatoes. Cook for a minute. Remove from heat and add cheese. Keep aside.

Chapter 2: Other Low Fat Breakfast Recipes

3. In a bowl mix eggs, egg whites, salt and pepper and whisk well.

4. In a small non stick skillet heat olive oil and add half of the egg mixture. Cook slightly.

5. Tilt the pan so that the uncooked mixture will go under the cooked side. Cook for 1 minute and flip.

6. Add a ladle of the potato mixture on one side of the omelette. Fold the other side over this.

7. Cook on both sides properly.

8. Repeat to make more.

9. Garnish with favoured garnish.

Spinach Omelette

Ingredients

- 3 egg whites
- 1 tablespoon milk
- 1/2 teaspoon dried mixed herbs
- Ground black pepper
- 3/4 cup chopped baby spinach
- 1 tablespoon cheese, grated
- Salt
- Oil

Method

1. In a bowl mix egg whites, milk and herbs. Whisk.

2. Grease a skillet and heat it. Add the chopped spinach on it.

3. When the spinach starts to wilt pour the egg mixture. Allow to set.

Low Fat Breakfast

4. When the edges are set gently lift them to allow the remaining liquid run underneath.

5. When set add the cheese and fold the omelette.

6. Serve hot.

Frittatas with Smoked Gouda

Ingredients

- 2 teaspoons olive oil
- 1/3 cup chopped onion
- 4 cups packed baby spinach leaves
- 2 cups sliced mushrooms
- 4 large egg whites
- 2 large eggs
- 1/2 cup shredded cheese
- Salt
- Pepper
- Oil

Method

1. Keep the oven on preheat mode at 350 degrees F.

2. Heat a large non-stick pan and grease it. Add the mushrooms and onions and sauté for a bit.

3. Cook till the mushrooms are tender. Add spinach and cook till it gets wilted.

4. Take a medium sized bowl and add egg whites, eggs, salt, cheese and pepper. Whisk.

5. Pour this mixture in a greased baking pan.

6. Add the spinach and mushroom mixture. Sprinkle the

Chapter 2: Other Low Fat Breakfast Recipes

remaining cheese.

7. Bake for 30 minutes or until done.

8. Cut into 4 wedges and serve.

Breakfast braid

Ingredients

- 1 pack pizza crust dough (refrigerated)
- Oil
- 1 tablespoon olive oil
- 4 ounces chicken sausage, chopped
- 1/4 cup onions (chopped)
- Jalapeño peppers, chopped
- 2 large eggs, lightly beaten
- 1/4 cup shredded cheddar cheese
- 1/2 cup Cottage cheese, shredded
- 1 large egg white, whisked

Method

1. Keep the oven on preheat mode at 425 degree F

2. Put half of the dough in a greased baking pan and pat it down properly.

3. Grease a skillet and heat it over medium heat. Add the sausage chunks and onions and cook till brown. Now slowly add the eggs and cook till set. Keep aside.

4. Sprinkle the cottage cheese lengthwise in the centre of the dough and leave the sides. Pour the egg mixture over this cheese.

5. Sprinkle cheddar on the top and finally add jalapeño.

Low Fat Breakfast

6. Now cut the border in to 2 inch diagonal cuts and arrange these strips over the filling diagonally. Press ends under to seal.

7. Lightly coat with egg whites for shine.

8. Bake at 425° for 15 minutes or till done.

9. Keep aside for five minutes and slice and serve.

Whole Wheat Pancakes

Ingredients

- 1 cup whole wheat flour
- 1/2 teaspoon baking soda
- 1 teaspoon baking powder
- Salt
- 1 cup low-fat buttermilk
- 1 egg, lightly whisked
- 2 tablespoon honey

Method

1. Take a large mixing bowl and add baking powder, baking soda, flour and whisk.

2. In another bowl add honey, egg and buttermilk. Whisk.

3. Combine the wet mix with the dry mix.

4. Let the batter rest for a couple of minutes.

5. Heat a greased girdle.

6. Ladle out some batter on this girdle and spread it on the girdle. Cook until edges get done. Flip. Cook. Repeat till done. Take out on a plate.

7. Repeat to make more pancakes.

Chapter 2: Other Low Fat Breakfast Recipes

8. Serve with jam or honey.

Sunny Frittatas

Ingredients

- 2 cups egg substitute
- 1/2 cup milk
- Salt
- Black pepper
- Oil
- 2/3 cup ham, diced
- 1/2 cup bell pepper, diced
- 1/2 cup green onions, sliced
- 1/4 cup cheddar cheese, shredded

Method

1. Keep the oven on preheat mode at 375 degrees Fahrenheit.
2. Mix the egg substitute, eggs, salt and pepper in a bowl and whisk.
3. Heat a medium sized skillet and grease it with oil.
4. Add the ham, onions and pepper, sauté for a couple of minutes.
5. Add the egg mixture and cook for around five minutes. Stir occasionally.
6. Add cheese. Take off from heat.
7. Pour this in a baking tray and bake at 375 degrees for 12 minutes or until done.
8. Cut into 4 wedges.

Conclusion

We hope that this book will help you in cooking delicious, healthy and sumptuous breakfasts, which will make you and your family happy as well as fit.

All the recipes given in this book are tried and tested and all of them are nutritious as well as tasty. The smoothies section will definitely be popular amongst children, who are fussy about finishing their breakfast.

Finally, if you enjoyed this book, then I'd like to ask you for a favor, would you be kind enough to leave a review for this book on Amazon? It'd be greatly appreciated!

Printed in Great Britain
by Amazon